# I Love It

The Life and Remembrances of

Darin Lee Ping

By Larry Ross Ping

Published by
Spiritbuilding Publishers
9700 Ferry Road, Waynesville, Ohio 45068

I LOVE IT
The Life and Remembrances of Darin Lee Ping
By Larry Ross Ping

ISBN: 978-1955285-54-4

**Spiritbuilding**
PUBLISHERS

spiritbuilding.com

# Table of Contents

# *Dedication*

I related the things in this book with Darin always being in the forefront of my thoughts.

But, at the same time, I never forgot my four sisters and many other family members.
I also realized that I, my four sisters and Darin came to be because of two other people. Mom and Dad.

Through God's eternal plan, they were the two responsible for Charlene, Rosie, Peggy, Jenny, Darin, and me being born into this world.

Mom and Dad were the ones who taught us right from wrong, respect of other people, the necessity of hard work and, foremost, love of God. The two of them provided godly examples to all of us. Darin became the boy, the man, the person he was because of all that they did for him.

I continue trying to live my life as God's word directs but I also remember the love they showed to me and the example of godly living. Their influence was immense, and I dedicate this book to their memory.

I pray that I will always have the ability to remember them.

# Foreword

God has richly blessed us in many ways. In September of 1965, God blessed humanity with the advent of Darin Lee Ping, a truly special individual. But in many ways, special isn't the right word. Then again, there isn't an optimum word to describe Darin. He was just, like they say, one of a kind.

His smile was infectious. His humor, apparent. And, his kindness—unsurpassed. He was truly a great guy that is missed by countless family members along with hundreds of others who were blessed to know him.

In this book, my dad does a superb job of sharing some memories of his baby brother and my uncle. You'll be laughing at Darin's antics, then crying as you realize how much you miss him. And for those that didn't know Darin, you'll come to learn about a man of 55 years who was and is an inspiration to so many.

Simply put, when it comes to the book you're about to read, you'll agree with Darin and with me—*I Love It!*

# Chapter 1

W e were a family. We were a family, that is, a father, a mother and five children, four girls and one boy. Dad was Roscoe T. Ping, born June 12, 1921. Mom was Mildred B. Long Ping, born October 13, 1924. They were married June 19, 1943, in Kentucky where they lived.

Barbara Charlene Ping was born September 14, 1944, in Willailla, KY. Mom, Dad, and Charlene (she went by her middle name mostly) moved to Indiana where Dad was hoping to find gainful employment. I, Larry Ross Ping, was born April 20, 1946. Roseanna Faye Ping was born March 6, 1948. Peggy Lynn Ping was born December 5, 1949. Jennifer Kay Ping was born June 20, 1955.

The seven of us were a family, a family of very modest means in a material sense but rich in love for one another. We rarely said, "I love you" but the love was there. Dad's love for Mom was abundantly seen in his everyday interactions with her. Mom, in turn, loved Dad and showed great affection for him. It was through Dad's love for Mom, his way of helping her when needed and just the apparent

everyday affection he showed that taught me how a husband should treat his wife.

We were all taught and shown by Mom and Dad's examples that God's word was all important in our lives. We always knew that the first day of the week, Sunday, was a day of worship. We also were very aware of how important it is for Christians to assemble, not only on the first day but also for Wednesday night Bible studies and gospel meetings.

God was first in our lives, and I believe I can state that all my sisters would say the same thing today. My four sisters and I were all baptized during our growing up years. Dad worked at a meat processing plant early on and into the 1950s, a job that paid very little, especially true with a growing family. But, for most of his working life, he was at RCA on the east side of Indianapolis. Living in various locations of Hendricks County, Indiana, the drive was long and the pay made making ends meet difficult. He remained at RCA for over thirty years with the last few years at a plant on the west side of Indianapolis, making the drive to work every day much easier.

Dad was committed to performing the tasks of his job. He had Mom and five children to feed, clothe and take care of. He truly was a "family man" and we were a family, the seven of us.

# Chapter 2

B efore Roseanna was born, Charlene and I were the only children. We played together, got in trouble together and hid behind the couch together when we thought we were in trouble with Mom or Dad. Those were good times, as I think about them now, and the memories are rich.

Rosie came along and I, as a three-year-old, don't have a lot of memory of her as a baby or little girl. I do recall one summer day, when we lived outside of Avon, Indiana, that Rosie had an accident. We lived in an old farmhouse and there were hogs in a lot next to the house. I remember hearing Rosie screaming suddenly. When I got to where she was, I thought the hogs must have run over her. I still don't really know what took place, but she had a broken arm and had to be taken to a hospital. But she healed and was fine.

I recall a time when we lived in the old farmhouse near Avon, a time that was not good for any of the family but a much more difficult time for our dad. Dad contracted tuberculosis in the middle to late 1950s. The TB meant that he could do nothing. He couldn't work, he couldn't provide for his own family. Yes, we had help from members of the church in Plainfield. We had help from Washington Township, from Hendricks County and the March of Dimes outfitted all my sisters and me with new clothing, including winter coats. The only humorous thing about this situation concerned Dad and his weight. He was always a small person and well fit. During the six months' recovery period, though, he began to put on extra weight around his waistline. Once he returned to work, he slimmed down again. His "having a stomach" was something I never saw on him again. This was a tough time but once again, we made it through. We were family!

# Chapter 3

Charlene, Rosie and I were close in age and were in very small schools together. More than once I had to deal with their broken hearts during the teenage years. Tears would flow when some boy would decide it was time to move on to another girl. Their broken hearts mended and both Rosie and Charlene eventually left their broken hearts in the past.

Peggy was the fourth child born and I don't remember a lot about her as a baby either. I do recall, however, incidents of her putting beans up her nose. That required some medical help to ease that problem. As I recall, and I think Charlene would back this up, the doctor said the beans had sprouted! Why would she do such a thing? I have no idea!

Following Peggy's birth, nearly six years passed before Jennifer came along. I was about nine years old, and I vividly remember Mom bringing her home from the hospital to the house near Avon. One day, Jenny was lying on a bed upstairs and I went up, knowing no one else was up there. As I looked at her, I thought she was the most beautiful sight I had ever seen. Her beauty brought me to kiss her over and over. I wanted to pick her up and hold her, but I didn't allow myself to do that for fear of dropping or hurting her. When she grew to school age, I would sometimes drive her to school. There was at least one time, though, that she couldn't "find" her shoes. The lost shoes were found where she had hidden them. She just didn't want to go to school that day!

There was also the time when I was taking Jenny down a slide, attached to a swing set we had in the yard. As she sat on my lap, we went down, hit the ground and she ended up with a broken collar bone. So much for a big brother taking care of his little sister. But she recovered and we were still a family!

The things I remember most about my four sisters were the *false* accusations that I tore up their dolls, even tearing the heads off the dolls. The absurdity of such claims cuts me deeply to this very day!

No matter the calamity, though, we were still family.

# Chapter 4

Dad's income was such that we always lived in a rented house and moved quite often. Then the time came in 1961 that Dad was able to buy his first house, located at 326 South Vine Street, Plainfield, Indiana. He bought it on contract from Nick Skelton, a member of the Plainfield church of Christ, where we attended. It was a big, two-story house with four bedrooms and two bathrooms, one of them being upstairs. I finally had my own bedroom, small but that was fine with me.

This big white house had a large front porch and with three pretty, teen-aged sisters, boys visited quite frequently! On occasion, there were some tense moments regarding these visitors, but everything worked out fine. Dad kept a close eye on that situation even to the point of chasing three boys up the stairs one night. He was chasing them because they had overstayed their allotted time. Where did those three romantics go once they were upstairs? They climbed out of an upstairs window onto the porch roof and jumped to the ground. They hit the ground running and were out of sight very quickly. Dad was a little late getting to bed that eventful night! I went to school at Plainfield with all three of those Romeos!

My sisters had to share bedrooms but there was more room than they had ever had before. Eventually, Dad built another bedroom and things were even better with that addition.

Wow! We had a house, lived in town, had space we had never had before, and everyone was happy although none of us wanted to leave Clayton High School and start anew at Plainfield.

# Chapter 5

Our house must have been more than 80 years old when Dad bought it and no doubt carried a lot of history. Our family added to that history, not necessarily including the three guys who escaped out an upstairs window. Another plus to this house was that the upstairs had two bedrooms, one bathroom and a small kitchen. So, it served as an apartment also. Charlene and Buddy, Rosie and Jim, Peggy and John and Linda and I all lived in that apartment after being married. No, all eight of us didn't live there at the same time! But it provided a first home for each of us four couples when we were newly married.

A perk to living in that apartment was that the landlord allowed us to live there for a very reasonable monthly rent. Humor aside, we were thankful for Dad and Mom allowing us to live upstairs. And we were a family!

# Chapter 6

Time was marching on. In 1962, Charlene graduated from Clayton High School and in 1963 she married Buddy Dorn. In 1964, I graduated from Plainfield High School and Rosie married Jim Cadwell in September 1965.

We were still a family but now had two brothers-in-law.

After high school, I decided not to go to college and found myself a job, a place I really liked and the place where I happened to meet a girl. This girl, Linda Roach, worked there part time and was a senior at Southport High School. The manager allowed Linda to work there since she had been his son's girlfriend for four years through high school. She and I met. We both had eyes for each other, but I was a little slow in making any sudden moves. Actually, I was a little slow in making any move at all! Eventually we went a couple of places together and a few months later we were married.

Though I loved the work, the atmosphere between my boss and me was not an easy thing to deal with every day. I left that company, went to another, spending over 35 years with Consolidated Freightways before they filed bankruptcy. I held many positions with CF and am very thankful to them for providing me the ability to raise our five children. On September 2, 2021, Linda and I passed 55 years of marriage. I already stated this, but Dad's example of a husband was an important part of my marriage to Linda.

# Chapter 7

I now move back in time to the end of 1964 and getting ready to move into 1965. By this time, Charlene is 20 years old, I am 18, Rosie is 16, Peggy is 15 and Jenny is nine.

As we leave 1964 behind and 1965 begins, we are still a family. Two have now left home and have their own families. I have a job now and still live at home but can help Mom and Dad financially to some extent. Peggy and Jenny are still in school in Plainfield. Though beginning to establish homes of our own, Dad, Mom, Charlene, me, Rosie, Peggy and Jenny are still a family of seven, a family with love for one another.

Peggy, Jenny and I were still home as we moved toward the year of 1965. Mom was now 40 years old, and Dad was 43 years old.

1965 arrives. I don't recall any real conversation with Mom or Dad but somewhere within the first three or four months of 1965, we all find out there's an approaching event that none of us expected. I suspect Dad and Mom were more astounded than any of us five kids.

Mom was pregnant and had a due date in September. To say the least, this was hard to comprehend. Yes, we all had probably heard of such things happening, but this is happening to our own Mom and Dad? To our own family? I'm going to be a brother again at the age of 19? Charlene will be 21 and a big sister again? Unbelievable!

But it was true, and our family was happy. Mom and Dad were going to have another son or daughter and the rest of us were going to have another brother or sister. God has been good to all of us and now was no different. Our family was growing once again, after ten years had passed since Jenny was born.

Did we all realize how well God had blessed us and how much more he was going to bless us in the future?
Perhaps not.

# Chapter 8

Spring and summer came and went. I don't remember but I am sure there was at least one baby shower for Mom and the new baby. No doubt the ladies from the Plainfield church of Christ were very generous with their gift giving.

I also do not recall any problems or issues with Mom's pregnancy. Everything went as it was supposed to, at least to my knowledge.

There was an additional workload on Mom and Dad because Rosie was planning her wedding for September 4, 1965, near to Mom's delivery time. As Rosie would later say regarding her own wedding plans while Mom was about to have a baby, "Teenagers don't have a lick of brains."

Rosie and Jim Cadwell's September 4, 1965, wedding went off without issue as Mom's delivery date was drawing near. Mom was more than ready for the baby to be born. I don't recall, however, any complaints from Mom during the nine months leading up to the baby's birth.

September 12, 1965—Mom went into labor! Charlene urged Mom to go to the hospital and she eventually did.

Then came Darin!

# Chapter 9

Darin Lee Ping was born that day, September 12, 1965, and life, as we knew it, changed. The change was not a negative change nor was it a burden for Mom to have another child to love and take care of. Dad continued working, still providing love, food, shelter, and care.

I was 19 years old when finally, after growing up with four sisters, I had a baby brother. Even though I was 19 years older, I thought I would still be young enough to teach him how to play basketball. Who knows? Maybe he would learn the game and be an even better player than I was! But then it wouldn't have taken much to attain that achievement.

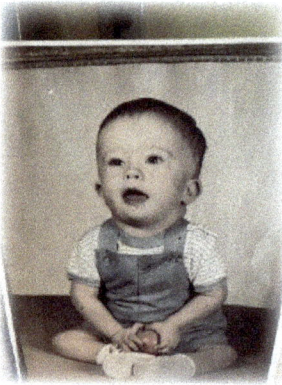

The days passed and all was normal as far as Mom and all of us were concerned. At some point though, probably two to three months into Darin's life, the doctors told Mom that Darin was not a normal child. In their terminology, Darin had Mongolism, a term that is now obsolete. Darin had Down syndrome, a condition that would not allow him to progress mentally and emotionally. He would not be able to do things other children would be able to do. Darin would have physical disabilities that would shorten his life span.

Learning to walk would come later for Darin. Someone told Mom that Darin might live to be a teenager, maybe even live to be 21 years old or so. Their expectations fell far short of how long Darin would live! Darin had a heart condition that would affect him for life as is the case for most Down syndrome children.

# Chapter 10

In addition to the information medical personnel had shared with my mom regarding Darin's longevity expectations, she also told me that doctors suggested Darin might be better off in an institution of some type, because Darin would require a great deal of care. I already knew Mom and Dad would never agree to any such thing happening.

Darin was a child just as the other five of us had been. Mom and Dad cared for us. They loved us. Why would Darin be thought of in any other way? After all, we were family! In years to come, Darin would state very emphatically and, on many occasions, "I love my family." He knew what family meant and expressed it with both words and actions!

Darin's life and other Down syndrome individuals reinforce the truth that their lives are of great value. In our own country, we have allowed millions of babies to be murdered. Abortion is legal. Whether our country deems murder of babies to be legal or not, God's law forbids it and says it is murder.

I am saddened daily knowing that these atrocities continue in our own United States of America. It should not be so! For those who knew Darin, can you imagine a world without Darin and others like Darin? I think not. That's as close to a sermon as I'll get but remember this. When a mother intends to kill her unborn baby and the mother or someone else carries out that intent, murder has taken place. Taking the life of a baby, inside the womb or outside the womb, is murder!

Darin was a son, brother, grandson, cousin, uncle, great uncle, nephew, and brother-in-law who unashamedly and without hesitation showed his affection. In fact, from the moment that he was born, he was an uncle to Charlene's oldest child, Kelli. That affection was extended to hundreds throughout

Darin's life, whether they were family, outside of our family or someone he may have met just five minutes before.

Having Down syndrome, Darin looked different than other individuals. We would notice people looking at Darin, some even pointing, when we were out in public. But where Darin's family went, he went. He was never left behind. He was never shunned. We were happy to have Darin, we were proud to be with him and Darin was, to my knowledge, never directly or personally belittled by anyone.

As he got older, he knew he was "different." He knew the word handicapped and he would say, on occasion, that he was handicapped. However, with his inability to pronounce words correctly, he would say he was "hersheycapped"!

Regardless of Darin's being "hersheycapped" or handicapped, he lived life to its fullest. Disappointments occurred in his life, but they were short-lived. If he wasn't happy, laughing or smiling, just wait a few minutes, at most, and he would then be smiling and laughing once again. Regardless of any reason Darin may have been down, he would quickly rebound and emphatically state, "I Love It." "I Love It" became Darin's life motto!

One thing that made Darin happy was food. People would say, "Boy, he must be a Ping. They know how to eat." Darin was no exception and his appetite allowed him to consume an enormous amount of food if not stopped. The fact that Mom was such a great cook certainly had an early effect on Darin's love of eating. At one point in his earlier years, probably in his twenties, his weight was near 300 pounds, much too dangerous. Eventually, he learned, with Rosie's help, how to control his ravenous appetite.

Darin loved eating, whether he ate at home or whether he went to a restaurant. He didn't like a great variety of foods and would, on many occasions, order a plain hamburger. If a place had fried chicken, mashed potatoes, gravy, and rolls, that would be his choice. Cracker Barrel was an exception. No matter what time of day he went to Cracker Barrel, his food selection was almost always the same, "mokehouse breakfast." Darin had trouble putting the "s" in the word smokehouse but that's what he wanted. "Smoke-house breakfast, scrambled eggs, turkey sausage, biscuits and gravy and orange juice."

Mom's words still ring in Linda's and my ears. Darin would sneak into the kitchen or, at least, he thought he had, and get a piece of bacon to eat. He loved bacon. Mom knew where he was and would say, "Darin Lee, you've had enough bacon." I think there were times when Darin had selective hearing!

When there was a birthday party, a wedding with food or any

family gathering, Darin was anxious to get there. He knew there would be food!

One thing we grew to expect from Darin on each visit was a handwritten note from him. I'm certain the same thing happened wherever he was visiting. He would take a scrap piece of paper, write on it, fold it up and place the note where it would be easily found. His note? "Out to eat." He loved going out but even if that didn't happen, he was happy. He rarely complained. One of his verbal expressions if told we were not going out was, "I wait," meaning okay, I'll wait until later. That's just another indication that he loved to eat and that he had the patience to wait.

# Chapter 11

As Darin grew older, he became quite a prankster. He loved playing tricks on someone and although the tricks were always the same as last time, Darin would laugh and have the greatest time performing these pranks. I must admit that he probably became a trickster due to his big brother's influence along with his love of The Three Stooges. "Pick out two"!

One trick he always pulled on me, and others too, carried a false sense of being nice and polite. Whenever I was getting ready to sit down at a dining table, Darin would come up behind me. I knew he was there but acted as if I didn't see him. He would say, "Let me get your chair for you, Sir." I would thank him graciously, begin to sit down and Darin would pull the chair away from me and I would fall to the floor. He would laugh uncontrollably then grab me and hug me, stating "I love you, Big Brother, you're crazy"!

Early on, maybe at the age of three or four, Darin nearly got me and himself in big trouble. Dad was taking a nap on the couch in the living room and Darin was climbing up and down while Dad slept. I was sitting in a chair across the room and doubled up my fist and made a motion for him to hit Dad. That was not too smart on my part, but I didn't think Darin would do anything. WRONG! Darin moved toward Dad's face, doubled up his fist and was ready to hit him with his best right hook. I jumped up from the chair, ran across the room, grabbing Darin just before he did any damage. Darin was a barrel of laughs, but I had to take care in what I was doing after that.

One more prank took place in the parking lot of our condo in Bradenton, Florida during Darin's last visit with us. Darin and I were standing next to a parking curb in front of our condo while Linda was using a water hose to water her plants. Darin kept trying to urge Linda to spray me with water. Finally, she did just that. Even though I knew the water was coming, it startled me. I tripped on the parking curb and fell on the asphalt. As I was going down, I thought to myself, this is going to hurt. But I was fine, no damage done. After I stood up, I told Darin, this was his fault. He denied any part in it, saying "Rinda did it, Rinda did it."

Both me and my sisters could fill many pages with more stories about Darin's playful attitude!

# Chapter 12

Mom, Dad, and Darin decided to go with Linda and me along with our children to Gatlinburg, Tennessee. We left in the afternoon which meant we would have to stop at a motel overnight. We pulled up to a place and made arrangements for two rooms. That was a mistake. We would all have to walk upstairs to get to our rooms. This was not good. Darin didn't do stairs. He was scared to death of stairs. We pleaded with him. We showed him how we would help him get up the stairs. Darin was having none of it. We pulled out all stops to persuade him and told him that in the morning we'll have biscuits and gravy. That was all to no avail. After a little while, one of us walked to the back side of this motel, seeing it was on a small hill, a hill that just maybe Darin could walk up and put him into the motel. Sure enough, Darin was able to do just that, getting him into the motel. Darin had several things he was hesitant to do. He had a fear of elevators and escalators. Many times, though, once he had overcome one of his fears, he would spread his arms and say, as if he never had a fear in his life, "E-A-S-Y." I don't remember if he did this with the motel incident or not, but it very well could have been one of those times.

There is such a thing as payback and Darin got his in 1993 or 1994. Darin, along with Mom and Dad, Linda and I and our children were at Jenny and Jim's in Boca Raton. No doubt our five children were in on this as well as probably David and Rachel, Jenny's children. Darin had gone to bed. Sometime after that all the kids decided they would pull a prank on Darin. They took numerous empty snack bags (chips, candy, Cheetos, etc.), and Coke cans and put them all around Darin on the bed where he was sleeping. I don't know the exact sequence of events, but Mom went into Darin's bedroom the next morning, saw all those empty snack bags, and said, "Darin Lee" and Darin was speechless. He tried to tell Mom he didn't eat all those snacks and he didn't put those empty bags on his bed. Eventually, she knew the truth of the matter, and everybody had a big laugh, even Darin!

Darin was allowed to have fun, pull pranks, and entertain anyone who happened to be around. Darin was also expected to show proper behavior. Mom and Dad taught Darin through proper discipline, and he accepted all that as most children will. There was never a time, in my remembrance, when Darin was upset because of any discipline that might have been administered. Just as I and my sisters were taught proper behavior, Darin was too.

As happens in any family, there were times of sadness. In November of 1995, Dad was undergoing surgery for lung cancer. There were complications during surgery and Dad never regained consciousness. He passed away on November 3, 1995, at the age of 74, a sad occasion for all of us, Darin being no exception. Our family was now reduced to seven. Darin would speak about Dad often, telling stories and relating things that we all knew about and some things we didn't. We could always count on Darin to recall things that we would not. Darin's memory was astounding.

# Chapter 13

I made mention of Darin and his having a nice touch shooting the basketball. When he was in school at West Central Joint Services in Bridgeport, he was on the basketball team. The team traveled to Terre Haute for a game and Darin was describing how he did. With great excitement, he told me how he had dribbled the ball, how he had made passes and how he had done shooting the basketball. He went on in great detail for some time and I finally asked him who won the game. After the description he had given me with all his exuberance, he very simply, sadly and matter-of-factly answered my question by saying, "I lost."

His nephew Leland, in addition to his being a preacher, is also a basketball referee. On one occasion, Darin was with Linda and me as we visited Leland and his wife Wendy. Leland had a high school game to referee, and we all went to the game in Murfreesboro, Tennessee. At halftime, younger children were allowed on the floor to shoot baskets. Certainly, Darin had to take part in that. Soon, everyone's attention was focused on Darin as he attempted to shoot the basketball from just inside the foul line. But shot after shot failed to go through the basket and a teenage boy kept giving the ball back to Darin. The whole crowd was cheering for Darin. Finally, after multiple attempts were made, Darin made a basket and the crowd erupted in cheers. Darin was wearing a University of Tennessee sweatshirt and immediately, after hitting the shot, he began running toward the opposite end of the court in celebration. The crowd was standing and applauding. Darin moved toward the crowd and many people in the crowd began high-fiving Darin. He was loving it and the crowd loved him. He was so excited, and it was a moment many people will not forget.

Among other terms attributed to Darin, he was unforgettable. This event occurred a couple years before Darin's passing. For sure, Linda, Wendy and I will never forget the excitement he generated that night.

As I think about Darin wearing the UT sweatshirt, I am reminded of Darin's loyalty to different schools and sporting teams. When he stayed with his sister Jenny and her husband Jim in Boca Raton, Florida, he was loyal to Purdue where both Jenny and Jim had gone to school. Darin was in a day care facility while Jenny and Jim were working in the daytime. On Thursday, the school kids all went bowling and wore their bowling shirts. Darin made sure Jenny had his bowling shirt clean for each Thursday.

When he visited his sister Peggy and her husband John in North Carolina, he was loyal to the University of North Carolina and wore his UNC shirts. At home with Rosie and Jim, he was loyal to the Colts, the Pacers, IU, and Purdue. He wore the appropriate hat or shirt when they had a game on TV.

One other indication of his loyalty was centered about his "Grandpa Roach" who was in the Army and served his country in

World War II, receiving the Purple Heart for wounds he received in Italy. Darin was a loyal Army man!

During Darin's last visit with us in Florida, he was there when the annual Army versus Navy game was being played. Linda arranged an Army/Navy pizza party and invited two couples we have known through the years. Bill and Pat are from Hobart and Nashville, Indiana. Our other friends, John and Joyce, are from Hobart, Indiana. Darin made preparation for the Army football game against Navy by getting an Army haircut.

He also wore his Army hat and shirt for the occasion.

Darin became great friends with John and Joyce but gave them the thumbs down sign because they were Navy fans. Not only were they Navy fans but they were both Navy veterans. Even after the party, whenever Darin saw them at church, he would give them the thumb down sign to remind them he was an Army fan.

Was Darin a loyal person? Most certainly he was, and his loyalty was spread far and wide, depending where he was and who was around at the time. Loyalty: another memorable characteristic Darin had.

# Chapter 14

There was no doubt, Darin was an entertainer. He loved being in front of an audience and had no fear, no stage fright! He would lead "Jesus Loves Me" before an assembly in a worship service. He was ready to make a speech at the drop of a hat. If it was someone's birthday, he had a birthday speech. If there was a wedding anniversary, he had an anniversary speech. Following Mom and Dad's passing, his speeches always included remembrances of them and that brought tears to everyone's eyes including Darin's. He loved entertaining but he always was respectful during times of sadness or seriousness. I don't think I've mentioned this, but Darin was intelligent, talented and adapted to different situations as necessity dictated. I'll have more about his intelligence later.

Indeed, Darin loved entertaining and standing before a crowd. Darin had a passion for entertaining. He was able to do impressions of many TV and movie actors.

He would impersonate George Burns. He learned to speak like George Burns and even pretended to have a cigar in his hand while his audience laughed and applauded.

Another was Gomer Pyle. In fact, he impersonated Gomer Pyle, USMC, and Sergeant Carter. Darin would do the Gomer Pyle walk, moving side to side, and then do the unmistakable voice of Sgt. Carter. "I can't hear you; I can't hear you, you Knuckle Head, you." And then "Move it, Move it, Move it." Darin had his voice down to a science.

John Wayne's "Hold it right there, Pilgrim," James Cagney's "You Dirty Rat" and many more were in Darin's repertoire of impressions.

Darin received many requests but everyone who knew Darin knew Elvis was at the top of Darin's impersonations. From "Love me Tender" to "Heartbreak Hotel" to "Hound Dog" to "Jailhouse Rock" and beyond, Darin loved doing Elvis. Not only did he love it, he *was* Elvis Presley and told people just that. He could sing his songs while including Elvis' facial expressions, his movements, even down to Elvis holding his two fingers up toward the end of a performance. Darin could excite his audience while swinging his arm round and round as Elvis did.

Darin learned about Elvis, and other entertainers, by almost constantly watching videos. Without realizing it, Darin was studying hour after hour, learning all there was to know about so many famous people.

Darin loved being Elvis but . . . Elvis has left the building!

# Chapter 15

Earlier in this writing I stated Darin was intelligent and he was. Darin went to school for some time and learned how to read. He was very good at sounding out words and reading sentences. He may not have had every word correctly pronounced but he did well. Going to school helped him but I believe his level of education and intelligence was enhanced by his family. Whatever we, as his family were involved in, he was right there with us. He participated in many activities with us. We helped him understand news reports he might see on TV. He knew who the current president was and knew about current events going on throughout the world. He loved watching TV and, later, all the videos he had accumulated during his life. All these things contributed to Darin's intelligence level.

One such example of Darin being taken wherever we went occurred when Darin was only about ten months old. I wanted to take Mom and Dad on vacation to Hollywood, Florida where Mom's mother and father lived. Obviously, the distance from Plainfield to Hollywood, Florida didn't allow them to see each other often. So, we planned the trip for July 1966, not exactly the coolest month of the year to be in south Florida. Linda and I were not yet married but she also went on this vacation trip with us. Everyone was concerned with whether Darin, at ten months old and having Down syndrome, should be making such a long trip. All of us hoped we were making the correct decision. Darin's doctor seemed to think that Darin would be alright.

So, on a warm afternoon in Plainfield, we departed and headed south. Mom, Dad, Jenny, Linda, Darin and I were on the way in my 1963 Chevrolet Impala SS convertible. Darin spent some of his time in the boot of the convertible top with Mom sitting in the seat very close to him. The worry from all of us was that Darin would get sick. That didn't happen. I believe we had crossed the state line into Kentucky when Mom got sick. She had taken some iron tablets on an empty stomach and vomited, violently, and we had to stop. The only place we found was a gas station that would best be described as dilapidated with extremely dirty facilities. Well, we weathered that disaster and continued on. By the way, Darin was resting quite comfortably!

We were still in the first evening of travel when we arrived in Bowling Green, Kentucky. Darin was doing very well, no problems, no issues with him.

We couldn't get through Bowling Green before sickness struck again. This time, it was Linda. We stopped alongside the road in a residential area. Dad and I got Linda out of the car and helped her lie down on the grass in someone's yard. Immediately, two or three ladies came outside from their houses. I don't really know their nationality, but their English was not spoken very well. They were trying to tell us what to do to make Linda's sickness subside. After a few minutes, she revived herself and felt some better. We went into a restaurant shortly after that and had our first meal on the road. Linda, not yet a daughter-in-law, would later speak of Dad's kindness in feeding her mashed potatoes. Mom and Linda's sickness were now in the rear-view mirror. We didn't stop until we got to Chattanooga.

Before getting to Chattanooga, I began to get sleepy, nearly missed a turn in the road and decided to pull over and sleep for a while in the car rather than stop for the night. As Linda recalls this stop for "sleep," was for only 15 minutes when I said it was time to go again and away we went. 15 minutes must not have been adequate time to sleep?

The remainder of our Florida trip was without incident except for a problem with the car that cost about $300 for repairs! Ouch!

We were able to visit with my grandmother, grandfather, an aunt and uncle, see the ocean and feel the July heat in south Florida. There was no reason to have worried about Darin. He had a great trip.

# Chapter 16

Darin, as I mentioned, had fears of doing certain things but he also had an adventuresome side, at least sometimes. One year when Darin was probably in his teen years, Linda and I took Darin to the Indiana State Fair. Of course, we had to make a visit to the midway. There was a roller coaster that Darin wanted to ride. This roller coaster was built somewhat on the order of a Wild Mouse. Not using better judgment, I took Darin on the coaster. All was well until we started up the first hill and Darin became scared. He wanted off, he wanted it to stop, he was crying. I told him we couldn't stop, we would be okay, "close your eyes," I told him. He was not alone in being scared. So was I but my fear was because I had agreed to take him on this ride. Through the turns, up and down the hills we went and both of us survived but Darin was mad at me. Darin would retell this story for years and always putting the blame on me, rightly so, and related this experience with his anger toward me. Then he would laugh and hug me. What a great time the two of us had.

In another incident during a trip to Gatlinburg, Tennessee, Darin decided he wanted to take a ski-lift to the top of the mountain and ride the Alpine Slide down. Riding instructions were very simple. To slow the sled down, pull back on the stick. To speed the sled up, push the stick forward. There were two tracks and Darin was supposed to have waited on me. But, before I could get in my sled, he pushed his stick forward as far as it would go, and he was around the first turn, full speed ahead. That's the last I saw of him. I couldn't catch him. Once again, I had fears because I knew there were some very sharp turns and the last time I saw

Darin, he was at full speed. As I was within a quarter mile of the finish, I came around a turn and saw a sled off the track turned upside down and someone lying on the ground beside the sled. Yes, it was Darin. Linda had started up the mountain because she, too, felt something was wrong. We got to the accident site to find Darin with a torn jacket sleeve, a few scratches on his arm and hand but all in all, he was alright. We took him to get first aid, but he was alright. Through the following years, Darin would retell his story of the Alpine Slide and he demonstrated with great drama and body movements of just what transpired during his speed breaking trip down the mountain.

Darin was able to relate the details of all experiences he, and others, encountered during his lifetime. He had a tremendous memory although he might have used just a bit of embellishment in retelling some of those experiences. He did have a memory that exceeded anyone else's in the family.

There was an occasion one day while I was working at Consolidated Freightways. My office was on the second floor with stairs leading to my office. Darin, as I already mentioned, was afraid to climb stairs but Linda brought him up one day. She was able to coax him up the stairs. He came through the door into my office and proceeded to sit down in my chair behind the desk. I sat in a chair on the other side of the desk and Darin became the "boss." After a few words from Darin about my job performance, he said, "What do you want?" I stated to him, "I want a raise." His immediate reply, "Raise, raise, I'll show you a raise. You're fired." He then slammed his fist down on the desk!

As I think back, Darin was nearly a world traveler. That's a bit of a stretch but Darin, besides the Gatlinburg trips and the Florida

trip, did other traveling as well. In 1967, Linda and I moved from
Plainfield to St. Louis where I had taken a job with Consolidated
Freightways. Darin, Mom and Dad went with us to St. Louis as I
had job interviews scheduled. Some two years later, the company
wanted to transfer me back to Indianapolis as the company was
expanding its operations. Darin was with us as we moved back
to Indianapolis. Dad had driven a truck to St. Louis to help with
some things we needed to load and move. Darin, Mom, and Linda
took care of Darin while Dad drove the truck and I drove the car
back to Indianapolis. At three years old, Darin did fine. He was a
traveler.

# Chapter 17

Late in 1973, the company offered me a promotion and transfer to Menlo Park, California. We had just lost a baby, a mental strain for Linda and it was not a good time for Linda to be traveling. This baby would have been our first boy and Mom and Dad's first grandson. But, not using my head, I accepted the transfer and promotion. My boss had even told me to wait until the spring if I wanted but my ambition and hardheadedness wouldn't allow me to use proper reasoning and logic.

The job I was transferred to in Menlo Park wasn't really what I thought it was going to be. Also, knowing Linda's health condition and her somewhat unhappiness, I knew I had made a mistake. I asked to be transferred back to Indianapolis. The company was more than gracious to me and always treated me well. They moved me back with no change in salary and benefits. We would be back among family.

So, in April 1974, knowing Mom and Dad would never see California, I arranged plane transportation for them and Darin to fly into San Francisco. By this time, Darin was eight years old. Once again, he made the flight without incident, as did Mom and Dad.

After a few days, we had everything packed and left the transportation of our household goods to the company. We left San Jose where we lived and headed in the direction of Los Angeles so we could take the southern route, by car, back to Indiana.

Somewhere in Arizona, Dad was doing the driving and got pulled over for speeding. He was given a warning ticket.

In Southwest Missouri I was driving, and I got pulled over for speeding. The trooper issued a ticket to me, and we had to go to Marshfield, a small town in Missouri. After a visit to the courthouse, I paid the fine and we were on our way.

One thing I haven't mentioned yet is that Linda was pregnant with our third child, Larry Ross Ping II. To say the least, she was not feeling well and as we continued through Missouri, she became very sick. I sped up, trying to get off the interstate and find a hospital. But, once again I got pulled over for speeding. The officer, after having seen the situation, let us go and told us to take the next exit to find medical assistance. By the time we made it to that exit, Linda was feeling better, so I put the pedal to the metal.

After contacting Linda's obstetrician, he advised her there was danger in continuing the trip by car. So, when we got to St. Louis, she and I got a flight home. Dad drove the car home. Mom, Dad, Darin, our daughters, Lori, and Lisa, all made the trip home without incident as did Linda and me. Once again, we had no need to have concern over Darin. He handled over 4,000 miles of travel with no problem at all.

I wrote all the above to make the point that Darin loved to travel but it was more than just that. His travels always took him to someone he loved, those in his family. His sisters were dear to him as well as their husbands. He visited with Charlene and Buddy in Martinsville and Freetown, Indiana. He visited with Peggy and John in Eden, North Carolina. He visited with Jenny and Jim in Boca Raton, Florida. And of course, Rosie was his second oldest sister and, along with her husband Jim, took care of Darin in Plainfield, Indiana. Darin dearly loved all four of his sisters and their husbands.

# Chapter 18

I asked each sister to share some special memory (so many memories), some special occasion or one of Darin's escapades. I am deeply thankful for the following contributions: Charlene, his oldest sister, wrote the following with love, devotion and feeling: Our Darin, to Larry & Linda. Darin, oh my what a baby, a young boy, and yes, a man in ways. I miss him so much and love him dearly. But for him he is in a glorious place.

I was twenty years old; Kelli was two, and Mom was giving birth to Darin. And we were all happy she had a boy.

What a great and wonderful person he grew up to be. With all his "I fooled you" sayings, hugs, "April fools," singing, notes, drawings, exercising, jokes, and "I Love You" and many more sayings. What a brother! Love You Darin, *Charlene.*

His second sister, Rosie, was his legal guardian. Along with Jim, her husband, they had Darin for 17 years. Rosie wrote the following:

> How do I put into words to describe the person that Darin was? He was the most thankful, grateful, and caring person that you would have ever known. But any of you whom have had the pleasure to meet or be with him already know how wonderful he was.

Jim and I were so blessed to have Darin for seventeen years as his guardian sister and brother-in-law. He was my brother, but the relationship became one of almost raising a son. Darin taught us, as he did many people, that every day was a beautiful day. It didn't matter if the sun was shining, or if it was raining or snowing, it was always a beautiful day. Every day was special to Darin as it should be to all of us. Darin was a teacher of patience, helping, the true measure of love and family. Darin truly loved his family.

He loved the get-togethers for birthdays, holidays or just being able to go and spend a few days with any of his family. He became, as Jim and I would call him, a gypsy, because he loved going from place to place. Darin was the most thoughtful person Jim, and I will ever know. He thanked me for every single thing I did for him, even when I would correct him. He would thank Jim and me often for caring for him. He often would look at Jim and would say, 'Thank you for helping me and being my best friend'. He often would call others his best friend and you can believe that he truly meant it. His love was like no one else. Darin taught both of us so many things.

Darin and I would have our disagreements on his having to be told what to do or not to do at times. There was never one time that Darin dishonored me or talked back to me as some children would do. Jim and Darin had a very special relationship. Darin would always agree with Jim as long as I wasn't around. Giving you a funny incident that happened often, Darin and I were having a disagreement around Jim. Jim would put his two cents' worth opinion by telling Darin, 'Your sister's a lunatic'. Darin would say back to him 'No Jim, you don't say that. Rosie is my sister and she's right'. I would go on about my chores in another room and could hear Darin talking to Jim, saying, 'you're right, Jim, my sister is a lunatic'. There were so many special little times that meant so much to us.

I could go on and on writing about all of them, but again, if you were one of the lucky ones to be acquainted with Darin, you've experienced them also.

Jim and I know now the times we took for granted with him and know even much more now what an honor it was to have Darin with us. If we could all be like Darin, what a wonderful world this could be.

His third oldest sister, Peggy, has not had good health for some time. She loved being able to have Darin visit with her and John. They had a great relationship and Darin always spoke with terms of great endearment toward Peggy. Peggy and John shared the details of an incident that occurred during one of Darin's visits.

John wrote, reflecting on their past times together but because of Peggy's illnesses, have not had much opportunity to see Darin the past few years. It was a very special time each year when Darin would visit them in North Carolina. Darin loved being at Peggy's for Thanksgiving. He would tell us about the turkey, mashed potatoes, gravy, rolls with butter and many other items. He really enjoyed his visits but especially so with Thanksgiving.

John wrote to me about a particular visit where an event took place clearly demonstrating the goodness of Darin regarding his care for the welfare of others. This example shows Darin's concern for his brother-in-law John Berlin. John, Peggy and Darin made a trip to a local shopping center, a trip John said he would never forget.

Peggy was walking beside Darin while Darin was pushing a shopping cart. John was walking behind Darin and decided to have some fun with him. John was playfully teasing Darin from behind and Darin lost his balance. He then took a fall, wrenching his left knee. Sitting on the floor, Darin let John and Peggy know how much pain he was in.

"Off to the ER we went," John stated. Darin's knee was examined and then x-rayed. Darin would have several weeks to mend. John said he was saddened that he had caused such injury to his "good friend."

Later, John learned from Peggy that Darin had continually been asking her why John was so sad all the time. John was concerned because he had caused Darin's injury. But Darin was more upset that John was mentally hurting. Darin had less concern over his own knee injury and well-being.

Finally, John stated, "That was like Darin." He was interested in the way others were doing and less of himself. "We miss Darin."

His fourth sister, Jenny wrote the following humorous story about Darin. "One of the funny stories showing Darin's quick wit is when he and Jim were out and Darin was riding his bike. We had got one of those low to ground bikes where he could pedal and feel safe when riding. He loved that bike. I think it gave him a feeling of independence. Jim would walk very fast along with him, as Darin would get going. They would just go back in the neighborhood behind us. One time they left on a ride and a Florida rain came up quickly, a soaking rain. I was watching for them to get back so I could have some towels ready. When I saw them approaching, I grabbed a couple of beach towels. I went to open the overhead garage door so they could get in faster, and there was Darin standing, laughing so hard he could hardly contain himself. He was soaked from head to toe, water dripping everywhere, even from his glasses. He was laughing so hard he could hardly talk, looked directly at me and said, 'Jenny, pass the soap', continually giggling the whole time.

Jenny also wrote, "Darin loved going to his school, as he called it, to see his friends. The first time I took him there, I didn't leave him. We just stayed there for a while and let him meet everyone. This was a day care center that had Down syndrome children. A lot were his age and had physical handicaps. There was a range in age, but most were younger. He loved it. They had reading classes, arts and crafts, went bowling once a week and went to the library once a week. They had movie days too."

The biggest thing was music days, which Darin always took over, but they didn't mind. They loved watching him sing and act out Elvis. They always had a great Halloween party that Darin loved where everyone dressed up. This place was the one and only place that I think Darin went by himself and made him feel somewhat normal. He even would help all the handicap.

The staff there and all the volunteers loved him. His favorite thing there though was going bowling. They all had bowling shirts they wore every Thursday. He always made sure I had that shirt clean. In the beginning, I had only meant for him to go part time, but he was adamant about going every day. I couldn't bribe him with anything to miss a day.

My wife Linda loved Darin as if he were her own brother and when Darin visited us, she treated him as royalty. I want to share one memorable story that took place when we lived in Greenwood, Indiana.

We had been involved in an automobile accident caused by an alcohol impaired driver of a pickup truck who rear-ended us. As a result of this, Linda was undergoing physical therapy. I was still working at that time; Darin was with us, and he went with her to one of her therapy sessions.

Before she went to the therapy room, she told Darin to sit in a chair in the waiting room. He had paper, pencils, and other things with him to occupy his time. "Don't move until I get back," she told him. His reply was, "I won't."

After finishing her physical therapy, she went back to the waiting room where she had left Darin. Guess what?! Darin was nowhere to be found. Linda inquired of employees as to whether they had seen Darin or not. Yes, they had seen him but none of them had seen him get up from the chair.

There was a passage of time but the search failed as to the whereabouts of Darin. Panic set in. Had he gone outside? Perhaps he was trying to find his way back to our condo?

The facility had a maze of hallways and doors leading to many and various places. By this time, several people were involved in the search for Darin.

All of a sudden, a door opened, and Darin walked in without any sign of confusion. Darin asked Linda, "Rinda, where were you?" Linda asked Darin the same question and he simply said, "Restroom." Even those who worked there had no idea what restroom he would have found but somehow, he discovered a restroom in a location unknown to the people working there.

All this was just another example of Darin indicating there was no big deal. There was no humor in all that took place that day, but it has brought a lot of laughter in the years following the incident. Darin was oblivious to all the concern and worry he generated that day in Greenwood.

I extend my thanks and gratitude to my four sisters, their husbands and Linda, my wife, for their contributions to this book. As I read the words my sisters wrote and think about Darin being lost, I couldn't help but smile at some of Darin's escapades. I also realize the loss that each one feels knowing that Darin is gone from our presence but certainly not from our memories.

As the author, I also want to take the liberty to relate some of the experiences of Darin's last visit with Linda and me in Florida.

On November 27, 2019, a cold, blustery day in Indiana, Linda and I met Rosie and her daughter Kim in Martinsville, Indiana. Darin was also with them, and this meeting place was to take Darin back to Florida with us. So, we packed his belongings with ours and, indeed, we had a full load, but we knew this was going to be an adventure. Darin was excited about going to Florida and this turned out to be his last time to visit with us. Three months passed quickly.

We didn't tell Darin but our destination on that first day was Murfreesboro, Tennessee, where we were going to spend a few days with Leland and Wendy.

# Chapter 19

After a few hours driving, we arrived at Leland's house. Wendy and Leland came out of the house to greet us as we arrived. Darin had no idea where we were until he saw Leland and, in his excitement, he got mixed up. When he saw Leland, he exclaimed, "Larry Ross, what are you doing here?" It took a few minutes before Darin actually came to the realization that he was at Leland's house, not Larry's. This was just one of many comical moments with Darin although he didn't intend it to be that way.

As was always the case with Darin, he was happy and satisfied to see his nephew and his nephew's wife.

The next day was Thanksgiving Day, and we were all invited to Bill and Julie Bain's house for Thanksgiving dinner. The Bains are members of the Northfield Boulevard church of Christ where Leland is the preacher. Their hospitality and bountiful dinner were more than we could have ever expected.

Several people were at the dinner including Megan, Julie Bain's unmarried sister. No surprise but Darin was in love again and he said he was going to marry Megan. The wedding didn't happen, and, in fact, Megan is now married and her new name is Megan Bruce. It was a wonderful afternoon of food, talk and a great time associating with godly people.

Our few days with Leland and Wendy ended much too soon but we had a great time. Darin loved visiting, loved eating out and he would talk about his experiences there for some time to come, including the standing ovation he received for hitting the basketball shot in Murfreesboro.

On to Bradenton, Florida!

We left Murfreesboro at a time that would allow us to stop at one of our favorite restaurants en route to Florida. Darin knew nothing about those plans, but we made it to The Varsity Restaurant in Atlanta. This restaurant is very close to the Georgia Tech campus and is sometimes very crowded. Darin had never been to The Varsity and was ready to eat. As we walked up to the large service area to order our food, we were met with someone saying, "What'll you have, what'll you have?"

They have a variety of burgers and hot dogs and they are all good! So, we had hot dogs and hamburgers for lunch along with onion rings, fries, and sodas to drink. As was common, Darin's response was a simple yet meaningful, "I love it."

So, with that finished, we got back into the car and Darin was ready to move on toward Florida, still wearing his University of Tennessee sweatshirt. Traversing through Atlanta is not a favorite thing for Linda to do but with my driving expertise, we zipped right through on I–75 without mishap. We spent one night on the road and arrived in Bradenton on November 30, 2019.

# Chapter 20

Our days and nights were filled with activities including activities for Darin, a couple of doctor appointments for Linda and me and lunch out most every day. Linda provided great meals for dinner. Darin and I would both agree with that. Also, Darin was quite the proper gentleman as always, assisting me with my seat at the dinner table.

I had an ongoing issue with my voice and throat. This became an aggravating issue, especially leading singing at Cortez Florida church of Christ. After visiting my Ear, Nose and Throat physician, she sent me to a speech therapist, hoping that might help me overcome this issue. Darin went into the office with Linda and me to see the speech therapist, a young and proficient therapist. One of the things she wanted me to do was perform trills. She attempted showing and instructing me how to do this, but I was a failure at that. Darin sat in the room, quiet for the most part. But, once Darin knew that I couldn't do as the therapist wanted, Darin stood up and said he would show me how to perform the trills. Without any difficulty, he "trilled" away. The therapist was amazed. I tried again but to no avail. Darin sat back down and said in the way only Darin could, "Easy, Larry." I tried to do the trills at home and Darin would try and teach me how to do it, but I just couldn't do it. Darin's ease at "trilling" was a surprise to Linda, me, and the therapist.

# Chapter 21

C hristmas was drawing close and there were a lot of places we wanted to take Darin. One such place was UTC mall (University Town Center). There was a large outdoor section filled with Christmas decorations, food vendors, a train to ride around the Christmas village and all of it geared toward Darin's liking.

We had a great Christmas day and Darin received the gifts he wanted except for the one gift he had requested from Linda when they were shopping earlier. He had told Linda he wanted, "Spenders." Unable to accurately understand what he was saying, Linda asked again what he wanted. More emphatically, he said, "You know, '*spenders*.'" Linda asked for more clarification and for him to show what he wanted, and he said, while using a flipping motion with his thumbs on his shoulders, said "Spenders" again. Finally, Linda got it—Suspenders, she asked? You got it, he responded.

Disappointingly, Linda couldn't locate suspenders and forgot about Darin's request. Until, however, Darin's birthday came around later in the year. While on the phone with Darin, Linda asked what he wanted for his birthday. "Rinda," Darin said with a sense of frustration, "You know, 'spenders.'" Linda and I made it our goal to find suspenders. Thankfully we found them and gave it to him for what would be the last birthday gift we would give him.

Without question, Darin's visit to Disney was the highlight of his time with us in late 2019 and January of 2020. Linda and I wanted to take him to Disney World, so we made reservations at Pop Century for four nights. Of course, we made sure we were on the ground floor. I didn't want to have to promise biscuits and gravy again!

Darin was so happy that we had the first-floor room. We went to our room, he picked out his bed and was so excited and exclaimed, "I Love It!"

The next morning was Sunday and, as was usual, Darin was up early and had himself dressed and ready for worship services. We went to Fortune Road church of Christ in Kissimmee, Florida. Linda and I were formerly members there when we lived in Kissimmee. So, we worshiped with many friends that Sunday and one member was gracious enough to provide Darin with a pass to the Magic Kingdom. We had a wonderful time being with old friends on that Sunday.

We decided to go to The Catfish Place for lunch in St. Cloud, just a short distance from the church building. Darin would never order any kind of fish or seafood. He ordered fried chicken and mashed potatoes and had a great lunch. Once again, as he was finishing his lunch, he said, "I Love It." After the evening worship service, Darin was anxious to get back to his room and to his work. He had coloring, drawing and plenty of things to do before he finished up his Sunday.

Early on Monday morning, January 13, 2020, we made our way to Magic Kingdom! The first order of business was to obtain a wheelchair for Darin. We needed to make it as easy as possible for

Darin to be able to get around while he was there.

It was a wonderfully magic day for all of us. We all had a great time, but we know Darin was more than just pleased to be there. He was thrilled!

He rode the teacups and helped me spin the cup as fast as possible. He laughed so hard I had to do most of the spinning work!

Probably his most favorite ride was Dumbo, so much so that he rode Dumbo twice.

He was greatly excited to see Buzz Lightyear and was very happy to meet him. Linda was able to get a picture of the two of them together.

Among other rides, he loved the Tomorrowland Speedway. I did the driving, but he kept wanting me to catch up with the car in front of us and "bump him."

Riding a roller coaster was out. I think his previous experience from years ago when I rode with him at the Indiana State Fair was his first and last roller coaster ride.

The three of us greatly enjoyed the entire day and we made many memories together!

Darin was one who was always easy to satisfy. He was fine just staying around Pop Century and I believe his greatest enjoyment, outside of Magic Kingdom, was spending the evenings in our room. He would sit on his bed with all his accessories right there with him. He would write. He would color. Of course, Darin wanted his snacks right at his bedside while he was working. When he got tired and was ready to go to sleep for the night, he would gather all his papers, his pencils, and any other things he had out and neatly store them in their proper places. He never lost his desire for neatness.

On Tuesday, January 14, we spent our day around Pop Century and Disney Springs.

We spent time in the evening having dinner at Port Orleans, Riverside, the place where Darin did his freehanded drawings of Mickey Mouse. We had that drawing framed along with two pictures he colored of Mickey Mouse. One of the Disney cast members assisted Darin by finding coloring pages for him to use and that was the inspiration for him to do his free-handed drawing at that time.

To this point, Darin had not gotten a souvenir but that was soon to change as he and Linda went into the gift shop at Riverside. Much to my dismay, and following a lot of looking, Darin found his perfect Mickey Mouse with a pennant attached. The pennant read, "Walt Disney World" and Darin was so happy with his choice. We bought Mickey for him. He was so happy with that choice and while he was in the dining room, he would place Mickey in front of his face and would then verbally mimic

Mickey's voice as entertainment for people nearby. He continued to do that throughout the rest of the time he was with us. Mickey was always with him!

Sadly, on January 15, we all had to return to Bradenton and our Disney vacation was now a memory.

Shortly after returning home, Darin received a card from his pal Mickey Mouse. It was a thank you from Mickey thanking the Ping family for spending their 2020 vacation at Disney World. Linda and I were happy to have been with Darin on this trip. The memories are lasting and we're thankful for the time spent with Darin.

It was time for Darin to leave us, but he was not leaving Florida. Instead, he was moving on to south Florida for his next destination. He was looking forward to visiting with his sister, Jenny, and his brother-in-law Jim in Boca Raton, Florida. Darin's excitement was also heightened by the fact that he would be seeing his school friends he had made through the years.

Linda and I arranged a meeting point and met Jenny and Jim. Darin continued his traveling with them. It was no coincidence that this was not just any meeting point. We met at a Cracker Barrel, Darin enjoyed his meal and his traveling continued. As I said before, Ricky Nelson would have been proud of Darin, The Traveling Man!

# Chapter 22

In regard to his intelligence, and with a mental age of maybe eight years old, he knew a lot about the Bible. He may not have understood everything, but he heard many preachers in his lifetime. Dad taught him a lot about what it meant to be a godly person and eventually Darin wanted to be baptized. So, on July 6, 1983, Darin, not yet 18 years old was "buried with Him in baptism." Johnnie Edwards, the preacher, even issued a certificate showing the date that the baptism took place in the building where the Plainfield church of Christ met.

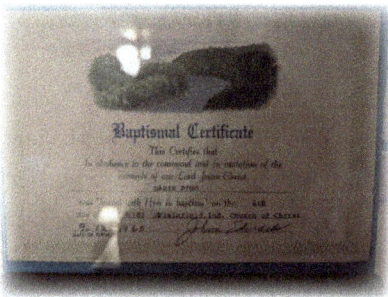

Although the song "Jesus Loves Me" is not exclusively a children's song, Darin loved to sing that song and even would lead this song during singing sessions when the church assembled. As I stated before, he had no fear of standing before an audience.

Darin was a caring person and was always ready and willing to help in whatever the situation was. Linda's dad, Sidney, was no

exception for Darin. Obviously, Sidney was not Darin's grandpa, but Darin always called him "Grandpa Roach." He wanted to help feed him, help him in a wheelchair and offered him many other acts of kindness. He visited Linda's dad with us many times at the nursing home in Mooresville, Indiana. Of course, Darin always knew that each visit in the middle of the day meant he would eat lunch with "Grandpa Roach." "Grandpa Roach" passed away on April 1, 2019, at the age of 97.

Darin grieved for his "Grandpa" and for Linda.

# Chapter 23

D arin loved his sisters, their husbands, their children and Linda and me. He loved his dad and loved his mom. It's hard to describe the magnitude of his love for Mom. He took care of Mom when she was sick. He was so sympathetic. He was so attentive! It would be an impossibility to relate all the things Darin did for Mom during the years following Dad's passing, things that many children would have left undone.

During the time they lived by themselves, a potentially dangerous situation occurred but turned out to be rather humorous. Darin or Mom had put something to eat in a toaster oven in the kitchen. After a while, Darin walked into the kitchen while Mom was sitting in a living room chair. As Darin walked into the kitchen, he stopped, turned back to Mom and stated very matter-of-factly and with no excitement, "Mom, the kitchen's on fire." Mom called 911, the fire was put out and no real harm came of that episode.

Darin was a traveler and loved visiting with his sisters and their families for weeks at a time. He spent time with Linda and me in Indiana and in Florida after we had moved there. One thing we could always depend on with Darin was his attention to neatness and cleanliness. Almost without exception, Darin would be up and out of bed before either of us. He would be dressed. He would have his bed made. He kept his clothes hung up or put into drawers as the case might be. He did all these things without being prodded. He just did it and I'm sure he did the same thing when he stayed with other people. Seeing Darin pay attention to details such as making his bed provides a lesson many others need to learn. Make your bed! Show a bit of interest in neatness! It's your house but, I'm just saying!

In addition to his morning routine of neatness and what became his normal routine, Darin was consistent in greeting the day. As he was already up and Linda and I might come into the room where he was sitting, Darin would say, "It's a beautiful day" or "It's a beautiful morning." He might even say something about the beauty throughout the day. He recognized things many of us take for granted. Sunday was no different. He would be up, fully dressed with coat and tie, ready to go to worship services.

His neatness was also noted in other aspects of his life. Darin loved to write but more than that, he was quite artistic. In the bedroom Darin used when he stayed with us in Florida, Linda has a display of some of his handiwork. Most of this relates to Disney World where Darin had such a wonderful time when visiting with us. There are pictures he has colored but also a free-handed drawn Mickey Mouse with the words, "Walt Disney World" printed on it.

Single handedly, Darin has used enough paper in his lifetime that would have eliminated a small forest of trees. Every time we would go shopping, Darin always wanted to buy a pad of paper or a notebook. Most of the time he would ask Linda, but it made no difference. I would have bought what he wanted. He was thrilled when we said okay, go ahead.

Darin had the ability to keep himself entertained with these activities I've written about. He wrote poems, notes, and letters. He watched videos daily, even in his last days while he was in the hospital, I'm told he watched his favorites. As Rosie told me on the phone, Darin didn't know he was sick.

During Darin's visits with us, he always kept me up to date on his latest girlfriend. I think he had a girl in every place he visited through the years. No doubt, Darin's sisters and other family members recognized Darin as a real "ladies' man." He would state on some occasions he was going to get married. Of course, that was just Darin being the joking kind of person he was. Darin was especially drawn to a waitress at Cracker Barrel in Bradenton, Florida. He told her, on several occasions, he was going to marry her. She went right along with him as if she really was going to marry him. The waitress' name was Ludy. We happened to see her many months after Darin had last visited. She asked about Darin and wanted to know how he was. Sadly, we had to inform her of Darin's passing.

He visited with Linda and me in Greenwood and Nashville, Indiana as well as Bradenton, Florida. It was especially exciting for him to be with us, knowing he would be visiting Disney World and Mickey Mouse!

In addition to all the above-mentioned visits, Darin had many nieces and nephews, all of whom looked forward to having him come to their houses. Ricky Nelson would have been proud to have had Darin by his side when he sang, "I'm a Traveling Man." Darin was a traveler!

Once again, Darin loved his family, and we were family.

Darin expressed his love without reservation. Whether he was expressing his love for me, for Linda, one of his sisters, his brothers-in-law, his nieces, nephews or any other person, Darin gave his love completely. That love was especially true for Mom.

On each visit to Florida and his stay with us, he always told us he was going to move to Florida and be with us. I suspect he told everyone else the same thing and, at those times, I'm sure he meant it. Following Dad's death, Mom lived another nine years. Mom lived in the house on Vine Street all those years with Darin.

I previously stated that Darin, after Dad's passing, did so many things for Mom. Darin was his mother's son! If Mom needed something, Darin would get it for her, providing it was possible for him to have done so. Mom passed away on the morning of November 18, 2004, while in a hospice facility. Linda and I had Darin and were trying to get there quickly as we knew Mom's time was near. When we walked in, we were given word that mom had passed just a short while ago.

Rosie and Jenny were both with Mom when she passed. As Darin, Linda and I arrived, Rosie had Darin sit down in a chair outside of Mom's room. She went into detail about how sick Mom had been and gently trying to get to the point of telling Darin that Mom was gone.

In addition to Darin's intelligence, he also had great perception. After Rosie continued to talk to Darin, Darin interrupted her and said, "Has my mom passed away?" Rosie told Darin that she had. Darin then went into the room, sat down in a chair beside Mom's bed and "talked" with her for quite some time. He sang Jesus Loves Me and seemed satisfied when it became time to leave. Darin was his mother's son. Their relationship was as close as any earthly relationship could be. Darin was 39 years old when Mom passed on that November day in 2004. At age 39, Darin had already lived nearly two decades longer than doctors had predicted back in 1965. Darin and Mom's bond for each other was beyond real description. I would be thrilled if I had the words and descriptive terms to describe it to anyone who wanted to listen.

We would all do well to do everything possible to strengthen our earthly relationships and strive to have the relationship Darin had with his mother.

Darin now has a never-ending relationship with God the Father! With Dad's passing some nine years earlier and now Mom's, again our family had adjustments to make. The family we had and grew to be over the years was now different. We all felt the loss of both Mom and Dad. Yes, we had each other as brothers and sisters but we also had our own families and those growing up years were behind us. We had each other to lean on but distance, having separate families and many other factors made things different. But we were still family.

With Mom and Dad now gone, we took Darin to the cemetery whenever we could, placing flowers on the headstone. Darin's name was on the headstone also and he would say, " Some day I pass away." He knew the time would come. Rosie became Darin's legal guardian and Darin continued to live with Rosie and her husband, Jim, in Plainfield, still at 326 South Vine Street. While greatly missing his mother, Darin was happy. Rosie and Jim took good care of him, and Darin was able to visit with his brother and sisters for weeks at a time as well as his nieces, nephews, and their families.

Darin had a cat named Alex. One of the sad things coinciding with Mom's passing, was that Darin had to give Alex up. Linda and I took Alex and she even moved to Florida with us and also our cat Four Socks. Alex lived with us in Florida for several years but died at about age 18. Darin didn't know about that until we saw him some months later. He initially took that news calmly but a few minutes later burst into tears, grieving the loss he had just found out about. Darin would carry her many times and she would lie on her back in his arms as he talked about Alex, "my baby girl." Alex was his baby, and he took great care of her. Darin always had videos of his favorite artists. He loved the music and would sing along while he had his earphones on. He may not have always been singing "in tune" but he kept singing nonetheless and we had to listen to his version of the songs. I didn't mind it. I loved it. He was my baby brother!

# Chapter 24

D arin had open heart surgery some years ago but for the most part, he was rarely sick. Other than a cold, sore throat, sniffles, and things of that sort, he remained healthy during his lifetime. On Friday, April 9, 2021, Darin was not feeling well and related this to Rosie. He also didn't have an appetite which, of course, was not normal for Darin. Rosie thought he might have had Covid. Other than that, there was no apparent reason for his not feeling well. Using proper caution, Rosie took him to the emergency room. After a short time in the ER, he was admitted to the hospital for examination and testing.

He did have pneumonia, but his oxygen levels were good at the time.

Rosie had also brought Darin's earphones, his DVDs and his normal things for him to have just in case he was hospitalized. She told me in a phone conversation that Darin was just being Darin, watching videos and singing along with the music while he was in a hospital bed. Darin didn't know he was sick.

At some point, following some testing, it was determined that Darin had a form of leukemia. This news was not expected especially since he had not exhibited any real issues prior to his going to the hospital. Jenny was also at the hospital, having flown from Florida to be with Darin and Rosie. Doctors explained that this leukemia was common to Down syndrome individuals but most of the time this occurred in the early years of life. Although his levels were good, he was on oxygen. As time progressed, the levels decreased, and his oxygen intake was increased.

On Monday, April 11, Rosie and Jenny initiated a phone call to me and Linda. Darin was able to speak, and we had a short conversation. Before ending the conversation, Darin spoke directly to Linda. If you recall, I said earlier that Darin had difficulty pronouncing the L in Linda's name. He said, "Rinda, I have a surprise for you." Knowing what was coming, Linda asked Darin what the surprise was. He replied, "I'm coming to Florida." Both of us responded as we normally would have. We acted surprised and told him we were glad he was coming to Florida to visit us. The greatest thing about this conversation was simply the fact that we were able to speak to Darin. We were well aware Darin's recovery was in peril.

On Tuesday, April 12, 2021, Rosie and Jenny made a video call to Linda and me. Darin was in his hospital bed and appeared to have tubes and medical paraphernalia covering his face. He was hardly able to speak but did manage a wave that gave all indication that it took a great deal of strength for him to acknowledge us. He tried to speak although what he said was nearly inaudible. We believe he said, "I love you." Just a few seconds later in this morning conversation the call was ended.

The pneumonia had taken over almost all of Darin's ability to breathe even with the high levels of oxygen he was being given. Only a small space of one lung was left. I don't recall what time it was when we had the aforementioned conversation, but it was probably around mid-morning.

Just a few hours later, we found out that Darin took his last breath at 1:17 pm.

I speak for myself and Linda. I speak for our children, Lori, Lisa, Larry II, Leah, and Leland. I speak for my four sisters, Charlene, Rosie, Peggy, and Jenny. We felt an immense loss, knowing that Darin was no longer in this world. Darin would no longer laugh with us, no longer eat with us, no longer tell us corny jokes, no longer visit with us, no longer entertain us. I think back on what Mom had told me over 55 years ago. Darin might live to be a teenager or possibly to the age of 21. Well, Darin, you showed those experts, actually living 55 years and seven months!

The old cliche, gone but not forgotten, is certainly true, but with Darin, it seems especially true. God has blessed us all with the wonderful ability to remember. And, for as long as I have memory, Darin will truly not be forgotten.

I would love to take Darin to the Cracker Barrel for one more 'mokehouse breakfast'. I would love to stop at the next gas station and buy Darin a Nehi Orange drink. I would love to hear him sing Hound Dog one more time for me. I would love to hear him and visit with him in Florida once more. I would love to take him on another roller coaster. I would love to see him ride the Alpine Slide once more. How many more things could I mention?

Those memories will live on for all of us whether family or the many others who loved Darin during his 55 years on this earth. During the visitation at the funeral home, an old high school friend of mine told me, "You lost your buddy, didn't you?." Another told me, "You know, Darin's not a Down syndrome anymore." I did lose a buddy as did so many others. But it is true, he no longer has Down syndrome.

Darin's passing was our loss, his gain.

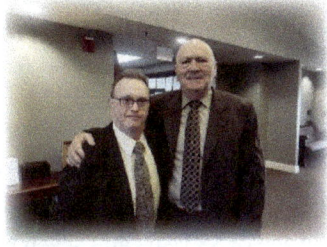

One thing I had never thought of until after the funeral, Darin lived at the same address all his life, 326 South Vine Street, Plainfield, Indiana 46168. Yes, he traveled quite extensively but that was home, the first and only house Dad bought back in 1961.

Now, Darin lives on in the place God has provided for all his children. He will live there for eternity. We all have an eternal spirit, never dying. Darin is in the hands of God and while I greatly miss him, I know he's happy.

If it were possible to ask Darin how he likes where he is, his answer, without hesitation would be—*"I love it!"*

# Final Thoughts

A s I write these thoughts, Darin has now been gone for over a year. He passed from this earthly life on April 13, 2021, at the age of 55 years and seven months.

Everyone loved Darin. My family loved Darin. There were various reasons as to why Darin was so well liked and so loved. He was a blessing to all who knew or met him in his lifetime. He was funny, comical, loving, caring, sympathetic, intelligent, and so many other adjectives could be used in describing Darin.

One thing, though, that dominates my mind about Darin is that, yes, he was all those previous mentioned things, but he was a teacher. How so? He taught us about love. He taught us that love is a natural thing. Darin loved me and had love for his brother that few people understand. He loved his sisters with great fervor. He loved his dad, knowing that a dad was to be the head of the household. He loved his mother, knowing she was the one with such great strength, the one who could advise, could be critical if necessary.

I am now over 76 years old and have seen many things through my lifetime. Darin was a most amazing person. I loved him as a brother, as a human being and as someone who set a great example as to the kind of person, I should work toward being. I loved Darin. I loved everything about him. I loved his life and all there was to Darin.

"I Love It"

Finally, I do want to acknowledge and thank those who contributed to this venture. Linda, my wife, has been a great motivator, helping me stay focused with my written thoughts of my brother, Darin. I also thank my sisters for their contributions. All of them, along with other family members, have provided encouragement in this endeavor. Thank you very much!